Edited by
ANTHONY NEWMAN

JOHANN SEBASTIAN BACH
The Well Tempered Clavier

Book Two

Ed. 3365

GREAT PERFORMER'S EDITION

G. SCHIRMER, *Inc.*

DISTRIBUTED BY

HAL•LEONARD®
CORPORATION
7777 W. BLUEMOUND RD. P.O. BOX 13819 MILWAUKEE, WI 53213

Contents

INTRODUCTORY NOTES

Meters, Tempos, and Accents

Basic to all questions of rhythm in Baroque music is the concept of alternations between "strong"and "weak," not only as it applies to individual notes, but as it extends to many different structural levels of music. This concept was taken for granted in all European music as far back as the 16th century. The Italians referred to *note buone* and *note cattive* (*good* and *bad* notes). They were also called "principal notes" or "passing notes." This strong/weak alternation underlies most of the specific considerations that follow: meters, accents, fingering, rubato, etc.

In spoken poetry, strong/weak are indicated by alterations of both volume and duration. Depending on the possibilities of each musical instrument, strong/weak patterns were indicated by alterations in either or both of these (for instance the symbols ⊓ and ∨ , used by string players to indicate bowing). Because the organ and harpsichord have no potential for dynamic alteration, the rhythmic alterations are of even greater importance.

It was taken for granted that a piece should rarely, if ever, be performed at a mechanically precise tempo from start to finish. Johann Mattheson wrote in 1731:

> . . . a row of tones which are perceived hastily and following one upon another affect the ear quite differently than if the same tones are presented slowly with good mediation [not only] of the tempo itself, but of the on-the-beat [good] notes ["anschlagende Noten"] in particular, and their relative importance. This tempo makes that which appears bad to be good, and that which appears to be good bad, depending on whether it is arranged short or long, fast or slow. [*Grosse General-Bass Schule*, p. 195]

These alterations within the tempo were absolutely essential in conveying the inner meaning of the music. The performer learned to recognize the strong/weak structures, important stressed beats, and deviations from the rhythmic norm. The musician's problem of applying this kind of insight to performance is similar to the task of the actor reading Shakespeare. The true meaning of the music could never be conveyed in strict time, especially on instruments with no possibilities for dynamic gradations, such as the organ and the harpsichord.

• • •

From the time of Frescobaldi through Bach, it was commonly understood that each metric signature had a specific accent pattern as well as inherent tempo.

One of the problems we encounter in Bach's music is that much of it has come down to us in copies made by people who were unaware of, or careless about time signature conventions. This is especially true of the use of the symbols C and ₵ , which were often copied interchangeably. However, properly understood, they designated different beat and speed patterns. At times engravers substituted C for ₵ at will, depending on whether or not they had a ₵ as part of their font. This has resulted in a serious misunderstanding of musical intentions regarding tempo and beat pattern in a number of pieces. When we examine manuscript copies, we have to determine whether it is Bach's own copy, that of a student faithful to Bach's understanding of the conventions, or that of a person who might not have understood the accepted practice.

If we find a manuscript with a ₵ , we can usually assume it to be correct since the most frequent copying error in the older manuscripts was to write C where ₵ was originally intended. I find it odd that none of the preludes and fugues from Book One employs ₵ with a 16th-note motion, a common occurrence in Bach signatures. So I question the reliability (at least in terms of signatures) of the important "autograph" copies. I would suggest a ₵ signature for the prelude in D Major (No. 5), and the fugues in C♯ Major (No. 3), E Major (No. 7), and g minor (No. 16) since they are livelier and faster in spirit.

Here are some excerpts from Johann Phillip Kirnberger, an important student of J.S. Bach (*Kunst des reinen Satzes* in der Musik, Berlin, 1774). [ ] indicate editor's comments:

Anyone can see at first glance that the most moving song would be robbed of all power and expression if one note were performed after the other according to no particular rules of speed, without accents and without pauses, even if the tones were played with the most precise purity. [P. 105, line 5 ff.]

Therefore it is movement, beat, and rhythm which give to a song its life and its power . . . [Line 17, ff.]

Every piece of dance music has its particular "beat movement" [*Taktbewegung*] which is determined by the meter and by the note values which are used within it . . . those with longer beats, such as the alla breve, 3/2 and 6/4, move more heavily and slowly than those with shorter beats such as the 2/4, 3/4 and 6/8, and these in turn are less lively than the 3/8 and 6/16 . . . a Loure in 3/2 has a slower beat movement than a minuet in 3/4, and this in turn is slower than a passepied in 3/8. With regard to note values, dance pieces using 16th's and 32nd's as the fastest note value have a slower beat movement than those using primarily 8th's with a few 16th's . . . a Sarabande in 3/4 has a slower beat movement than a minuet, even though they may both be written in the same meter. [In general, then, the larger the denominator of the signature, the faster the tempo.] [P. 106, line 28 ff., through p. 107, line 12]

Thus, the *tempo giusto is determined by the meter and by the length or shortness of the note values in a piece.* [P. 106, line 28 ff.]

Finally, the composer must not forget to indicate as precisely as possible the proper movement of his piece to the extent that it is not already determined by the above-named characteristics. He must use the words allegro assai, allegro moderato, poco allegro, etc., wherever the word allegro alone would make the tempo too fast or not fast enough; with slower pieces, the same would apply. The words which describe the characteristic movement, such as maestoso, scherzando, vivo, mesto, etc., are often of utmost importance and not to be treated lightly by one who wishes to perform the piece well. [P. 112, line 28 ff.]

It is exactly as with common speech, in which it is only through the use of accents and the length or shortness of syllables that we can make words and phrases distinguishable.

Meter consists of the exact uniformity of accents which are put onto a few tones, and in the completely regular distribution of long and short syllables. It is when these particular heavy or light accents re-occur on the same beats that a song receives its meter or beat. If these accents were not distributed regularly, creating the exact periodic repetition, then the song would resemble very common prose speech; through these periodic repetitions, however, it resembles verse which has its exact meter. [P. 113, line 23]

[about 2/2 or ₵, or alla breve] It is to be noted that this meter is very heavy and emphatic, but still it is to be performed at a speed indicated by the note values, unless the qualifying words grave, adagio, etc., specify a slower tempo. The same is true of the related 6/4 meter, of two triple beats, but the tempo giusto of this meter is somewhat more moderate. No note values smaller than 8th's may be used. [Four 8th's would then equal the beat.] [P. 118, line 18 ff.]

The 2/4 meter has the same movement as the alla breve, but is performed far more lightly. [I would infer "faster" also.] This difference between the performance of the two meters is so palpable that one could not possibly suppose it to be unimportant whether a piece is written in ₵ or in 2/4 [P. 118, line 18 ff.]

J.S. Bach and Couperin had their reasons when they wrote some of their pieces in 6/16. Who does not know the Bach fugue WTC II, *Fugue in F Major*? [P. 119, line 18. . .]

If it is re-written into 6/8, the movement is no longer the same, the pace is far heavier, the notes, at least the held ones, receive too much weight, in short, the expression of the whole piece suffers and is no longer the same as Bach put into it. [6/16 is lighter and faster than 6/8] [P. 120]

If this fugue is to be properly performed on the keyboard, the notes must be played with a light, fleeting movement without the slightest pressure; this is what the 6/16 notes indicate. On the violin, pieces in this and similar meters are to be performed only with the tip of the bow, but pieces in the heavier meters require a longer stroke and more pressure on the bow. [P. 120]

This must be said about these meters with two beats, that each measure consists of a foot with two parts, the first long and the second short, and that therefore the main note of a melody must fall on the first beat of the measure, as it is called, on the down beat. [Kirnberger calls our attention to the differences between strong and weak beats in a measure, and the strength of the down beat.] [P. 120, line 17]

The 4/4 meter, indicated by **C** , is of two kinds. It can be used instead of the 4/2 meter, just described, using the qualifying word grave, and is then called the "great 4/4 meter," or it is the so-called common even meter, also called the "little 4/4 meter."

The great 4/4 has an extremely heavy movement and expression, and because of its emphatic nature is used primarily in large pieces of church music, choruses and fugues; 8th's and a few groups of 16th's are its fastest note values. In order to distinguish it from the little 4/4, one should notate it with 4/4 instead of with **C** . These two meters have nothing in common with each other except their marking.

The little 4/4 has a more lively movement and is to be performed with far more lightness. It can use all note values up to 16th's and can be used in the most varied ways for all kinds of compositions.

The 12/8 meter with triple beats which is derived from the 4/4 has similar characteristics. Some of the older composers who were very particular about the performance of their compositions often used the marking 24/16 on pieces in 12/8 with mainly 16th notes, in order to indicate that the 16th's should be played *lightly* and *hastily* without the slightest pressure on the first note of each beat. These subtleties seem to be so unknown to today's composers and performers that they believe these meter markings to have been idiosyncracies of the old composers. [P. 122, line 30 ff.]

In the meters in 4, the first and third are long, also called "good beats," and the second and fourth are short, also called "bad beats." The first is heavier than the third. [Line 8 ff.]

Even though 3/2 (♩ ♩ ♩) and 6/4 (♩. ♩.) each contain six quarter notes, these two meters do not resemble each other because of the difference of the weight on each beat . . . old, good composers treated the Courante, which is usually set in 3/2, in such a way that the two meters are often confused with each other. [Line 18 ff.]

The 3/4 meter is not found in church music as often as the 3/2, because it is to be performed more lightly, but it is found in the most varied uses in chamber and theater music.

Its natural movement is that of a minuet and as such it cannot use too many 16th's in succession, and even less so, 32nd's. [P. 129, line 4 to 9]

One errs if one considers this meter, 9/8, to be simply a 3/4 with triplets: anyone who is at all competent as a performer knows that triplets in 3/4 must be played differently from 8th's in 9/8. The former are played very lightly without the slightest pressure on the last note, but the latter are played more heavily and with some weight on the last note. The former can never, or only seldom, accept a harmony on the last note, but the latter quite often. The former can accept no break in the 16th's, but the latter can easily do so. If both meters were not clearly different from each other, then all Gigues in 6/8 could just as well have been written in 2/4, 12/8 would be the same as **C**, and 6/8 the same as 2/4; anyone can easily see how senseless this would be by simply trying to put a Gigue into 12/8, or a 6/8 into **C** or 2/4.

The older composers used 18/16 with three triple beats when they wanted to indicate that the piece was to be performed lightly, fleetingly and without the slightest pressure on the first note of each beat.

The 3/8 meter has the lively movement of a Passepied; it is to be performed lightly, but not frivolously, and is used extensively in chamber and theater music.

The 9/16 meter with 3 triple beats, which derives from the 3/8, was often used by the older composers for gigue-like pieces which were to be performed with extremely lively and light movement; in today's music, however, it is no longer used. The 9/8 takes its place. [J.S. Bach occasionally uses this signature, i.e., the Gigue from *Partita 4 in D* for harpsichord.] [P. 130, line 7]

When 8th's are used in 3/4 meters, and 16th's in 3/8, then the first note of each group is long. [This would indicate holding the note slightly.]

[Comments on the "set-together" meters]

In even meters with two beats, and in triple meters, there are melodies in which it is clear that entire measures are alternately heavy and light, so that one feels an entire measure to consist of one beat. When the melody is so constructed that one feels the entire measure to be a single beat, then two measures must necessarily be set together to make a single one, with the first part being long and the second part short.

For if this setting-together did not occur, one would have a melody consisting only of heavy beats because of the necessary heaviness of the down beat. This would be just as offensive as a portion of speech which consisted only of words of one syllable, each of them accented. [This is a brilliant setting-forth and justification of strong and weak measure construction.] [P. 131, line 20]

This is the origin of the set-together meters, that is, the 4/4 which is put together from two single measures of 2/4, or the 6/8 which is put together from two single measures of 3/8, and so forth. [I have indicated these groupings with ①. ②. ③. ①.]

Actually, this setting-together only occurs so that the player can find the correct mode of performance and can play the second half of such a measure more lightly than the first. One can easily distinguish these meters from the others; for instance, the set-together 4/4 from the single common 4/4, in that the ending in the set-together ones fall quite naturally on the second half of the measure and only lasts for half a measure, whereas in common 4/4 this would not be at all possible. In the same way, the endings in the set-together 6/4 can fall on the fourth quarter, which would be quite impossible in single 6/4. [A great many Bach works have cadences on the second part of a 4/4 measure, i.e., *C Major Fugue*, WTC 1 (No. 1). We can assume, then, that they are written in this "set-together" manner.]

[Perhaps this "set-together" measure idea comes from the compositional need to have other than two-measure groupings, e.g., three-measure groupings.] The 4/4, reduced into two measures of 2/4, would allow a grouping of three measures of 2/4 to be easily perceived. This is proved in 4/4 time, where the cadence falls on the second half of the measure where, in fact, we have a grouping of three 2/4 [or the "set-together" type] measures. [P. 132]

(Translation by Dorothy Barnhouse)

[We can certainly deduce from Kirnberger that each signature has its own specific accent pattern, tempo character, and mood,—and that the added Italian and occasional French words change the meaning of the signature in some way.]

Strong and Weak

Strong/weak alternations underlie Baroque music at every structural level. As already stated, it is impossible to discuss meters, tempos, accents, fingering, rubato, or almost any other specific performance problem, without being aware of the constant presence of alternations between strong and weak ("good/bad" or "principal/passing" metric units). This is true whether we are talking about individual notes as subdivisions of the beat, about beats as subdivisions of the measure, or about measures and larger structural units within the piece. The origins of strong/weak occur in chant, groups of twos (SW) and threes (SWW), and their elongation as tenors of Renaissance music, where their larger groupings of twos and threes were referred to as *maximodus*. Although many sources assume this to be a logical extension of the concept of stressed and unstressed syllables of spoken poetry prominent in the beginnings of Baroque music, ca. 1600, Mattheson went further and said that "in music the possibilities for variation between strong and weak have many levels, compared to poetry which knows only a few". (*Der Vollkommene Kapellmeister,* p. 170, No. 49). Most of the German texts of Chorales show simple alternations of strong/weak, strong/weak, and this is indeed a common pattern of alternation found in the music of this period. We also find, as Mattheson suggested, enormous variations,—not only the predictable SWW, or SSW, SWWW or SSWW, but also pieces with strong and weak measures that follow each other in no particular regular combination.

The following quotation from Quantz gives performers quite specific information about the concept as applied to individual notes, but not measures:

> Here I must make a necesary comment about the length of time each note should be held. One must know how to make a difference in performance between the main notes, also called principal notes, or by the Italians, "good" notes, and the passing notes, also called by some foreigners "bad" notes. Wherever possible, the principal notes must be brought out more strongly than the passing notes. In order to follow this rule, the fastest notes in every piece in a moderate tempo, or even in an Adagio, even though they appear to have the same value, must be played somewhat unevenly; thus the principal notes of each figure, that is, the first, third, fifth and seventh will be held a little longer than the passing notes, that is, the second, fourth, sixth and eighth; but this holding of the notes should not make as big a difference as the writing of dots beside them would. [Quantz infers gentle — 3:2 — ratios.] When I say "the fastest notes," I mean: quarters in 3/2; eighths in 3/4, sixteenths in 3/8; eights in Alla breve; sixteenths or thirty-seconds in 2/4 or in common time: but only if there are no groups of notes that are faster, or once again as short, among them, as then these would have to be performed as described above. For example, if one played the eight sixteenth notes in the following examples slowly and equally,

> they would not sound as pleasing as they would if one played the first and third of each group of four somewhat longer and stronger than the second and fourth, [Quantz, *Versuch einer Anweisung, die Flöte traversiere zu Spielen,* Chap. 12]

Other Baroque sources, sometimes in connection with bowing instructions for stringed instruments, discuss the concept of strong and weak measures, not only of strong and weak notes within the measure. Kirnberger gives the best and most complete description of strong and weak measures.

Many sources indicate that strong notes or beginning notes of passages should be stretched in time, and, depending on the possibilities of the instrument, should be played louder.

Obviously a single performer will have more options and obligations in the use of these rhythmic alterations than will a group of performers. It is above all music written for the keyboard or for an unaccompanied string instrument that presents the performer with the problem of finding and distinguishing between the strong and weak structural elements. Performers in music using more than one or two players must, of course, be just as aware of the strong/weak alternations, but the rhythmic deviations will be smaller and fewer.

We have seen how to determine the strong and weak beats within the measure. How do we determine which measures are strong? In general, a measure is strong

(1) If the theme begins on a downbeat:

S. 538

(2) If there is a cadence in any part of the measure. However short measures, two by two, will often have the cadence "weak."

(3) If there is a chord on the downbeat of a measure in a thin texture. The chord sometimes takes more time than the measure allows:

Italian Concerto, S. 971

(4) If the texture of a measure is thicker than that of the measures preceding it:

Prelude in G Major, S. 541

(5) If the downbeat has an ornament:

Fantasia in g minor, S. 542

(6) If there is a large leap after the note on the downbeat or third beat:

English Suite in F Major, Prelude, S. 809

Italian Concerto, S. 971

(7) Dissonance will tend to be strong:

Partita No. 3 for Violin Solo, S. 1006

We determine which measures are weak in the following ways:

(1) If there is a tie from the previous measure onto or over the downbeat, the measure is generally weak:

English Suite No. 5, Prelude, S. 810

(2) If there is a series of sequences — for instance, a statement and three repetitions — the statement is strong, the first repetition is weak, the second repitition is strong, and the last repetition is weak. A statement with two repetitions would normally be SWW:

Toccata in d minor, S. 538

Fugue in C Major, S. 870

This example deviates from the normal accent pattern. Holding the third count of the second measure somewhat would then indicate the change of direction in the sequential pattern.

The following example is exceptional:

Toccata in F Major, S. 540

This shows the statement followed by five weak repetitions, because of their 7-6 descending series. A repetition series ascending by step motion will often have a "strong" effect.

(3) If the first measure material begins on a rest, that measure is weak:

WTC I

There are various ways to differentiate or highlight a strong measure. The most important one is to prolong the downbeat (or another important beat) somewhat. The actual duration of the held note will, of course, vary with the situation, but experiment with holding it for about the value of an additional 32nd note, presuming a context of 16th notes. The time that is added to make this accent is not subtracted elsewhere in the measure.

The approach to the held beat or note should be "rounded," i.e., very, very slightly retarded. I have indicated these points with the signs = (slight) and − (very slight). It should not be overdone − but be barely noticed by a sensitive listener.

It is often a good idea to add an ornament on some part of the downbeat chord so that the time needed for prolongation can be taken without the awkwardness which might be produced if one were simply to hold the chord. Interestingly enough, Mattheson refers to bad (weak) chords as those devoid of the slightest ornamentation.

If the downbeat accent in a strong measure has been displaced to some other beat, then the displaced accent receives the impetus of the strong measure and is treated just as if it were the actual downbeat of the measure. In general, then, the patterns one finds in Bach are (a) SW; (b) SWW, S(S)W, in 4/4 subdivided / / / / | / / / / | / / / / | / / / or hemiola (three in the time of two) at triple meter cadences.

It is evident that the principles governing these rhythmic alterations and freedoms are not exempt from gross exaggeration and misapplication. On the other hand, they must not be ignored or denied as they were for the many years when phrases such as "utmost precision," and "mathematical exactitude" were used to describe Bach's music. It is only when the above principles are applied that a work of this period can, in fact, achieve an artistic unity and focus.

Fringing

Another device for emphasis is called "fringing," a term first used by Roger North and recently reinstated by Sol Babitz. Fringing is useful for the emphasis of strong metrical units. Passages written to be played simultaneously are unsynchronized for emphasis, i.e., the notes of one hand are played slightly before or after the notes on the other hand, even if they appear to be written together. North described it as the mixing of the note with the one before or behind it "which doth not corrupt but rather fringes the tone . . . ." He also said that when two notes are played "to a tough together," nothing is achieved by the doubling but "a little loudness, but in the other way by frequent dissonances there is a pleasant seasoning obtained."

To achieve this effect play the bass slightly before the upper voice, i.e., the soprano can be played slightly late or the bass played slightly early. The delayed soprano is referred to by Couperin and other French writers as "suspension." (This has nothing to do with contrapuntal suspension.) The following example shows how and when this kind of fringing can be used:

WTC I, Prelude No. 2, S. 847

Fingering

The older combinations of finger patterns were usually limited to seven or eight consecutive notes in the same direction played with one hand. This would normally mean there would be one or two "scratch-overs" or "finger over finger" — for instance, a passage played by the right hand (1,2,3,4,3,4,3,4). One does not ordinarily find longer passages of scale-writing in the same direction in older music except in virtuoso music. When a longer passage of fast notes occurs in Bach, his manuscripts show that the stemming of the notes and the beams often changes to indicate that the passage is broken up between the two hands.

In this edition I have combined older fingering styles with more modern ones. Often two possibilities are given. The modern player is urged to experiment with the older "finger-over-finger" styles. Occasionally "jumped" fingering makes a slur not playable in a literal manner. In that case think of the slur as a musical phrase grouping.

Partita in G Major, S. 829:

Passing the thumb under is a basic element of keyboard technique today, but it was not common in Bach's time. The keys of the instruments were narrower and much shorter front to back. It would have been far more difficult to use this technique without having an undesirable accent or heaviness on the note played by the thumb. Even so, Bach undoubtedly used it, as can be seen from this passage.

Italian Concerto, Third Mvt., S. 971:

This passage would be almost impossible at a fast tempo without passing the thumb under. But, although Bach himself certainly used this technique in playing, he probably did not teach it to beginning students. The thumb was used occasionally on sharp or flat notes, since it was more important to keep the hand in one position than to try to avoid the use of the thumb on these notes.

Typical Slur Patterns:

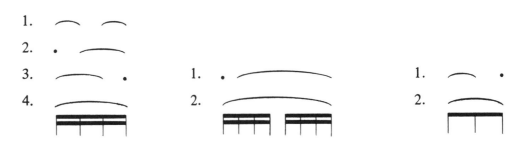

To ensure the emphasis of the downbeat, slurring often went across beats within the measure, rarely across the bar line. Proper articulation or realization of slurred groups is of the utmost importance in the realization of correct metric, signature, and rhythmic concepts of the 18th century. These considerations take precedence over the 19th-century "long line" concept. It is interesting to note that as the tempo increases, so does the necessity of slurred groups in keyboard music, since a detached style can only be played in moderate tempo.

Another articulation problem is the holding of notes through a texture to indicate voice leadings, especially in slower music, for example in allemandes. Also long notes (half and whole notes) were almost always played shorter than their written value.

Dotted Notes

Within certain limits evenly written notes should be performed as if they were dotted or similarly altered. This is not because the notational symbols used in dotting were unknown or unused, but merely as a labor-saving device employed when all music had to be copied by hand.

The notational convention of the Baroque for dotted notes is that the note(s) following the dotted note are equal to the value of the dot. However, the relative length of the notes and the dot was considered variable. Etienne Loulié, in his *Eléments ou principes de musique* (1696), an important French source on inequality, dotted notes, and other rhythmical questions, gives us several possibilities.

The Dot

Generally, a dot after a note increases its value by half. Often it adds to the note by 1/8, or 1/4, or 3/8, or 1/2, or 5/8, or 3/4, or 7/8. The dot of a quarter-note equals the value of a thirty-second note [A], a sixteenth-note [B], three thirty-second notes [C], an eighth-note [D], five thirty-second notes [E], three sixteenth-notes [F], or seven thirty-second notes [G].

So the figure written as ♩. ♪ could be played in any ratio from 𝄾𝄾𝄾 to ♩... ♬, depending on the context. But this does not mean that dotted notes always had to be realized in one of these varied ways. They could also be realized quite literally, again depending on the context.

C. P. E. Bach gives us an interesting rule. He said that with a group of eight 32nd notes the figure ♩. ♩ is played literally. Thus the following should not be overdotted.

WTC I, Fugue No. 5, S. 850:

The figure ♩ ♪♫. is almost always realized as ♪. ♪♫.

Passages that have ♫. against ♫ are sometimes realized together, both as ♫. or any of its variants.

Sometimes the figure will be played especially in overture textures.

(The reader is referred to Quantz, Chapter V, No. 21, for a detailed discussion of overdotting.)

This variability of note values in the realization of dotted rhythms, like the variability of the ratios in inequality, stems from the Baroque tradition of rhythmic flexibility.

Another problem is the figure  In slow-to-moderate tempo, the 16th will follow the last note of the triplet, as if it were the last in a group of six 16ths. In faster tempos the 16th will be played with the last note of the triplet, assimilated, as it were, into the rhythm.

In this example (fast tempo) the figures in question are beamed together.

Toccata in G Minor, S. 915:

Embellishments and Ornaments

The words "embellishment" and "ornament" are often used interchangeably today, but our use applies to two quite separate elements. Ornaments could be indicated by standardized notational signs, such as ᴧ or ᴧ, and there are many examples of tables which give exact directions for the realization of each ornamental sign. Cadence ornaments or , often omitted, were to be filled in by the performer. This often-cited table was given to Wilhelm Friedemann Bach by his father:

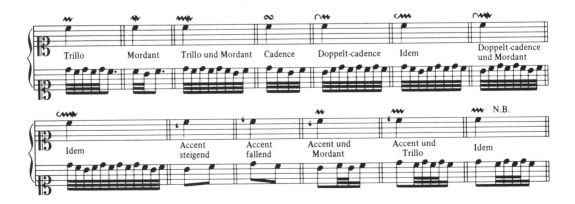

Embellishments, on the other hand, were decorations originally improvised by the performer. For instance, a passage written as

Sarabande from English Suite in g minor, S. 808

could be performed as

But another performer, or the same performer at a different time, might perform it as

A performer confronted with the ornamental sign 〰 would have no such freedom. The only notes he could possibly play would be

Ornaments punctuate; embellishments flower.

Ornamentation is possible in all voice parts. Normally, the top voice is most often ornamented, but all structurally important voices can be ornamented.. This is certainly necessary in the playing of fugues, where the fugue subject must be ornamented in the same place in all successive introductions of the material. This does *not* mean that the same ornament must necessarily be used each time, or even that the ornament should be of the same length as the initial one; Bach, for example, imitated short trills in the pedals. The ornamented area of the subject must be ornamented throughout the fugue, even if minimally.

The Realization of Ornaments

Trills (*tr* or 〰) should be played on the beat and for the most part from the upper note. If approached from the step above or if slurred from the previous tone, they will start on the principal note, before, on, or after the beat, depending on the context.

Trills can be shortened to a single appoggiatura, as mentioned by C. P. E. Bach.

Trill endings. There are two ways to end a trill:

(1) The trill stops before its note value ends; there is then a break (*point d'arrêt*), and the ending (*nachschlag*) or anticipation is added. This method is mentioned in many French ornament tables. Bach wrote a *Partita nach Fransösischer Art* in the Second Part of

the *Klavierübung*, in which he writes the trills with rests:

S. 831

(2) The other way to end a trill is with no such break before the ending. In such cases, the trill is written in one slur with its termination:

Schmücke dich, o Liebe Seele, S. 854:

It is better not to count the beats in a trill, or to practice counting them, unless it is a short trill.

Mordents (∿) are executed as follows:

The number of repetitions depends on the length of the note.

Appoggiaturas: The true appoggiatura is always on the beat. The Italian word tells us that the appoggiatura is leaning (slurred) onto the note following it. The length of the appoggiatura depends on the context. J. J. Quantz says that it should receive half the value of the main note, 2/3 if the main note is dotted. I believe that the long appoggiatura belongs to the newer "galant" style, and that J. S. Bach's style is short. The appoggiatura is always slurred into the next note and is slightly louder when played on an instrument capable of dynamic variations. It is sometimes shown as a small hook ⸜ or double hook ⸝ (circling the note), but most frequently as a small note.

In Bach's music we find instances where a small note treated as an appoggiatura would create parallel fifths if played on the beat. In these cases, I would play the small note before the beat.

The Canonic Variations of *Vom Himmel hoch*, S. 769:

One can play the length of the appoggiatura from 1/4 to 1/2 the value of the note to which it is attached, or 1/3 to 2/3 of a dotted note.

The *Schleifer* (two ascending steps, ⌒) may be played on or before the beat, depending on the context. French composers frequently write the *Schleifer* as two small notes before the main note, suggesting by the notation that it be played before the beat.

I have added dynamic suggestions (keyboard changes on a harpsichord) throughout the course of this work.

Anthony Newman

JOHANN SEBASTIAN BACH
The Well Tempered Clavier

Book Two

The Well-Tempered Clavier

Book II

Edited by Anthony Newman

1 Prelude

J. S. Bach

Fugue

a) Refers to "the strong" or important measures: see forward.

8

a) The editor plays the middle voice an octave higher until m. 76, then the entire notes in right hand an octave higher until the end.

2 Prelude

(repeat)

Fugue

3 Prelude

Fugue

a) The editor has filled in this type of thirds throughout the fugue.

4 Prelude

a) The editor plays the mordents in this way (a) and the appoggiatura, as 8th notes
(b) throughout the Prelude.

c) Trill in 32nds, or

a) Trill after the beat, on the main tone.

a) Trill in 16th note triplets, starting on F♯.

b) Trill after the beat.

Fugue

5 Prelude

a) The editor plays

a) The editor plays

a) ♩ ³♪ ♩ ³♪

Fugue

6 Prelude

a) These short slurs are from the manuscripts.

Fugue

a) The editor plays duplets in this fugue slightly dotted ♪. ♪ .

7 Prelude

a) Play appoggiaturas as 8th notes.

a) The editor adds a Roulade up to high A♭.

b) Trill after the beat, on main tone.

Fugue

8. Prelude

a) The editor fills in these and other thirds, ad lib.

Fugue

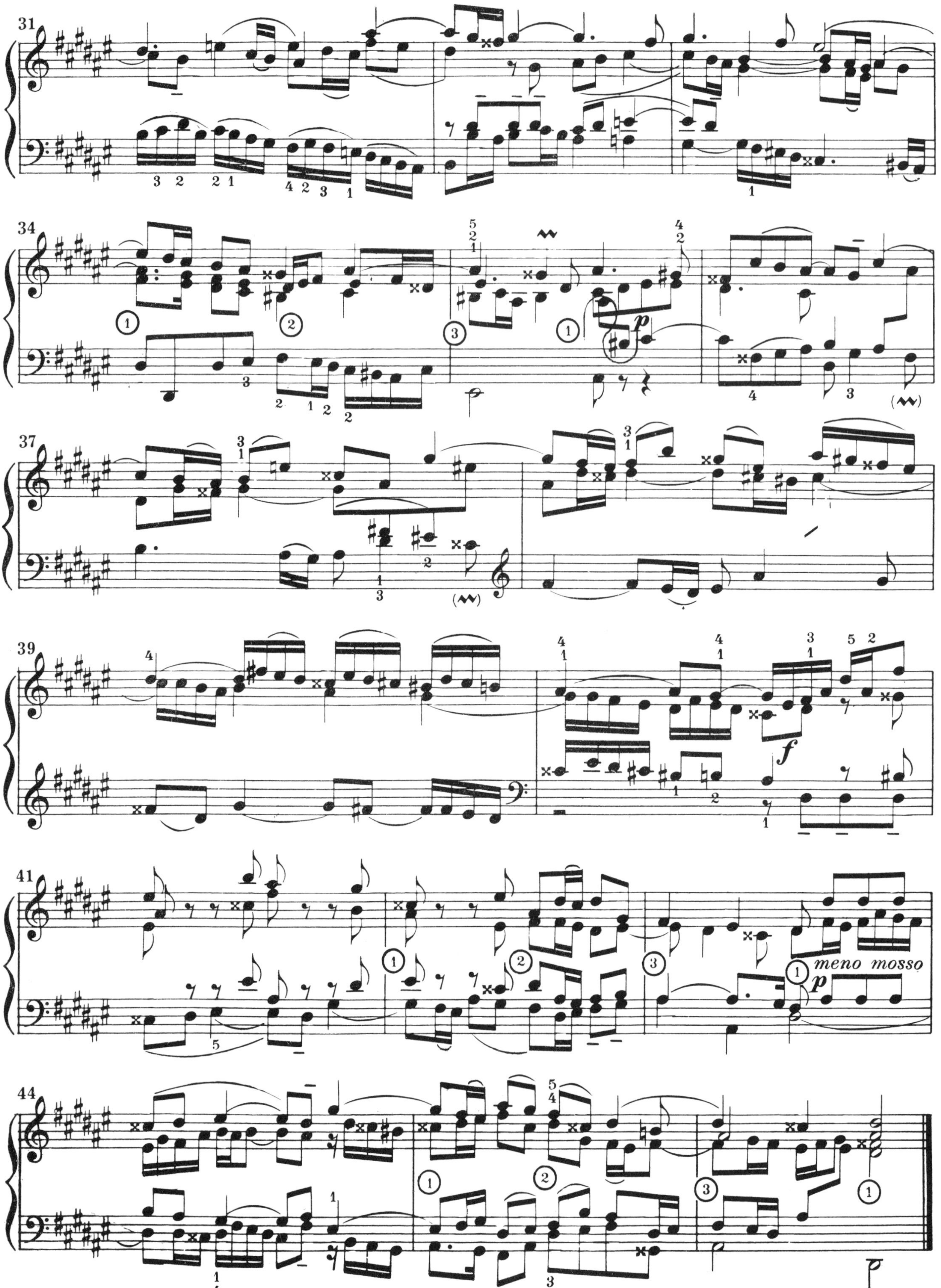
meno mosso

9 Prelude

Fugue

60

10 Prelude

a) The editor prefers the hemiola phrasing.

62

a) Trill before the beat.

Fugue

a) Wedges are found in the original.

a) Flourish

a) The last beat of a triplet

11 Prelude

a) Arpeggiate chords throughout, ad lib.

a) ♩ ♩.

Fugue

12 Prelude

Fugue

13 Prelude

a) 8th note

a) Trill in 32nd notes.

a) 8th note

a) Trill after the beat.

Fugue

a) Perform the long trills in this manner.

b) The following half notes in mm. 13-20 and mm. 44-50 form a long scalar motion.

14 Prelude

♩ = 40-50

a)

p

b)

a) 8th notes generally tenuto

b) The Prelude should be played rhapsodically with much rhythmic freedom.

(Più mosso)

a) Play 2 against 3

b) Short Flourish

Tempo primo

Fugue

a) Add trills, ad lib.

98

15 Prelude

Fugue

16 Prelude

a) The editor trills from the upper note.

(poco più mosso)

Tempo primo

Fugue

17 Prelude

a) The editor plays the figure for the most part overdotted.

a) Slurs found in the original.

a) Trill after the beat.

Fugue

a) Similar ornaments may be added throughout.

a) Add cadenza

18 Prelude

a) The editor favors 16th-note grace notes in the Prelude.

b) Original dynamics

a) Slurs found in the original.

Fugue

a) The two subjects continue here.

19 Prelude

a) 8th note

Fugue

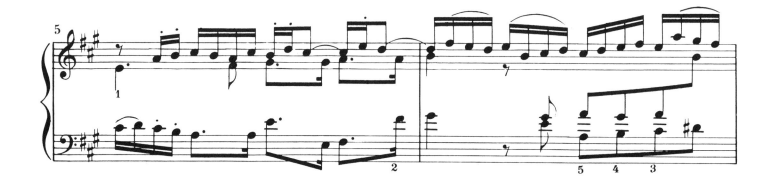

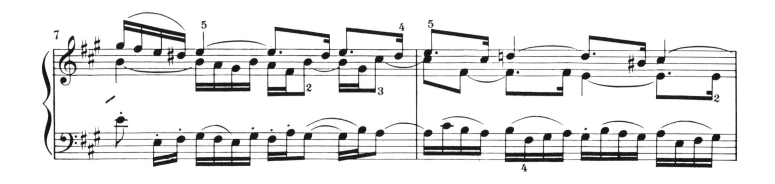

20 Prelude

a) Hold the harmony notes throughout the Prelude in this manner.

a) Start the trill on the 2nd half of the beat.

Fugue

a) Staccato marks found in the manuscripts.

b) Trill either

coll 8va - - - - - - - - - - - - - - - - ⌐ ⌐

(On Piano)

21 Prelude

Fugue

a) Slurs on 2nd and 3rd beats of mm. 3 and 4 are found in the original.

a) Play as a quarter note.

22 Prelude

Fugue

23 Prelude

158

a) Slides before the beat; apoggiaturas on the beat

Fugue

24 Prelude

Fugue